OW UP

# I'LL BE A FIREFIGHTER

BY CONNIE COLWELL MILLER    ILLUSTRATED BY SILVIA BARONCELLI

AMICUS ILLUSTRATED • RIVERSTREAM

AMICUS ILLUSTRATED is published by Amicus
P.O. Box 1329, Mankato, MN 56002
www.amicuspublishing.us

Paperback edition printed by RiverStream Publishing in arrangement with Amicus.
ISBN 978-1-62243-362-9 (paperback)

LIBRARY OF CONGRESS CATALOGING-IN-PUBLICATION DATA
Miller, Connie Colwell, 1976– author.
I'll be a firefighter / by Connie Colwell Miller ; illustrated by Silvia Baroncelli.
    pages cm. — (When I grow up ...)
 Summary: "Twins Lucy and Liam pretend to be firefighters after school and show
what it's like to be a professional firefighter"— Provided by publisher.
 ISBN 978-1-60753-761-8 (library binding) — ISBN 978-1-60753-860-8 (ebook)
1. Fire fighters—Juvenile literature. 2. Fire extinction—Juvenile literature.
I. Baroncelli, Silvia, illustrator. II. Title.
TH9148.M4535 2017
628.9'25023–dc23                                        2015029347

EDITOR        Rebecca Glaser
DESIGNER     Kathleen Petelinsek

Printed in the United States of America at
Corporate Graphics in North Mankato, Minnesota.

HC  10 9 8 7 6 5 4 3 2 1
PB  10 9 8 7 6 5 4 3 2 1

ABOUT THE AUTHOR
Connie Colwell Miller is a writer, reader, and teacher who lives in Mankato,
Minnesota. When she was little she always knew she would work with two things:
kids and books. Today, her dream has come true. She has written more than
80 books for kids, and she has four wonderful, creative children of her own.

ABOUT THE ILLUSTRATOR
Silvia Baroncelli has loved to draw since she was a child. She collaborates regularly
with publishers in drawing and graphic design from her home in Prato, Italy.
Her best collaborators are her four nephews, daughters Ginevra and Irene, and
organized husband Tommaso. Find out more about her at silviabaroncelli.it

… I am Firefighter Lucy! I work hard to keep the people in my town safe from smoke and fire. Whenever there is danger, Liam and I are there to help!

Beep! We hear the dispatcher's voice on our pagers. "Fire at 123 Broad Street. All firefighters report!"

I run to my locker. My heavy pants and boots are waiting. I step into them and pull them up. I grab my jacket and my helmet. Then, I run to the fire truck.

Every firefighter has a job to do. Liam drives the truck. He turns on the siren to tell other cars to get out of our way. I make a plan for when we get to the fire.

When we get to the house, we see flames and smoke coming out a window. The people who live in the house are standing on the sidewalk. They look scared. I ask them questions. "Is anyone stuck inside? Where did the fire start?"

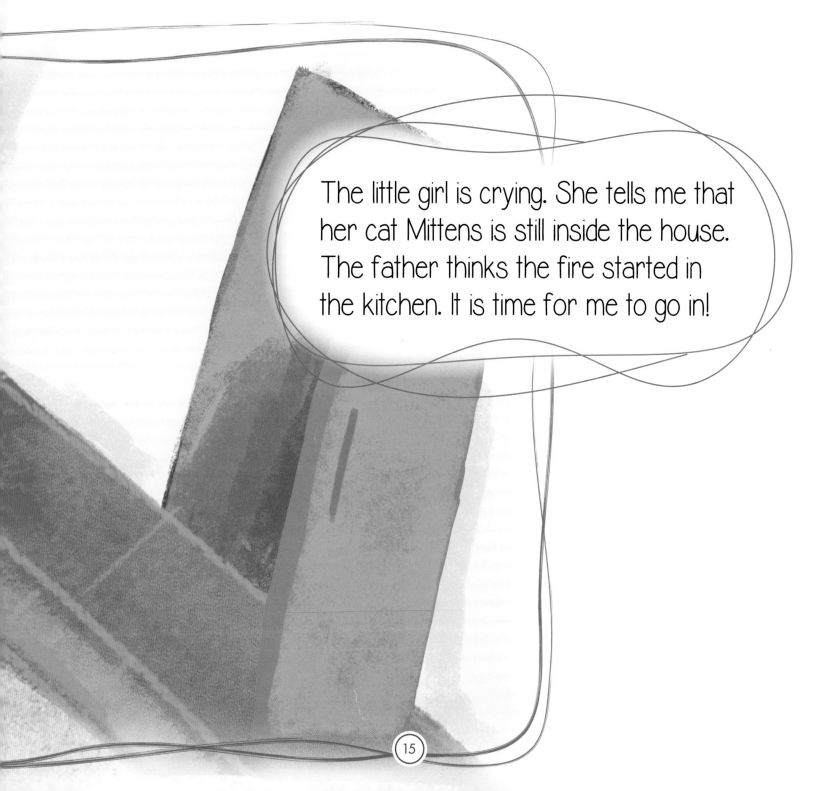

The little girl is crying. She tells me that her cat Mittens is still inside the house. The father thinks the fire started in the kitchen. It is time for me to go in!

Good news! This fire is small—only in the kitchen. I put it out with my fire extinguisher. And there's Mittens, hiding under the table.

Not all fires are this small. Sometimes we need to use the huge hoses and ladders from the fire truck. This time, we are lucky. And so is Mittens the cat!

The other firefighters and I return to the station. We check our gear and equipment. We have to be prepared for the next emergency.

## WORDS FIREFIGHTERS SHOULD KNOW

dispatcher–A person who takes emergency calls from people and then contacts the fire department for help.

fire extinguisher–A device used for putting out small fires; people keep them in their homes.

fire station–A building where firefighters work and keep their equipment, like fire trucks and uniforms.

helmet–Special headgear firefighters wear to protect them from smoke and heat.

pager–A device that allows a dispatcher to communicate with a firefighter in emergencies.

siren–A loud noise that a fire truck makes to notify people that a fire truck is coming and headed to an emergency site.

1. Using graph paper, draw a map of your home. Show all doors and windows.

2. Visit each room. Find two ways out.

3. Make sure you can open all windows and doors easily.

4. Make sure your home has working smoke alarms. Push the test button to make sure each one is working.

5. Pick a meeting place outside in front of your home.

6. Make sure everyone in your family knows to meet at this place in an emergency.

7. Make sure your house or building number can be seen from the street.

8. Learn the emergency phone number for your fire department.

9. Practice your fire safety plan!

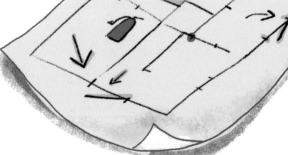